CONT

CW00531582

HOW TO USE THIS BOOK

Each walk (except loop walk 1) is accompanied by a section of the relevant Ordnance Survey Explorer series map, with the route marked on it. The key to the routes is given below.

▬▬▬▬▬▬▬▬	The Main Round
▬▬▬▬▬▬▬▬	The Loop Walks
● ● ● ● ● ● ●	Alternative route on Main Round

The main round and loop walks are marked with a distinctive waymarks shown below.

Where a loop walk follows the route of the main round, the route is only marked with the round waymark, and the instructions for the loop walk will direct you to the appropriate section of the main round.

Where a waymark is attached to a stile or a gate, cross the stile or go through the gate before following the direction indicated by the waymark, unless stated otherwise in the text.

Historical notes and points of interest are given in *italics*.

Stiles and gates. The footpaths in the local area are continually being improved and stiles replaced with gates. Hence, occasionally in the text reference will be made to a stile which has since been replaced with a gate.

Some of the paths can be wet and muddy in places, particularly in the winter or after heavy rain. Please be sure to wear appropriate clothing and footwear. Also, some of the paths are steep and can be slippery at times, so please take care.

The route description in this book starts at Backwell Lake, and follows the Round in an anti-clockwise direction. However, the Round can be joined at a number of places along its route. It is way marked in both directions.

If you are planning to start from the Lake, please remember that there is a time limit on the car park. At weekends there is usually plenty of parking in the nearby station car park. During the week, there is parking at the top of Bucklands Batch, in the direction of Nailsea, in Cheddar Close, which is accessed via Queens Road and The Perrings. Please park responsibly and with consideration for the residents.

THE NAILSEA ROUND

Around the outskirts of Nailsea - 9 miles

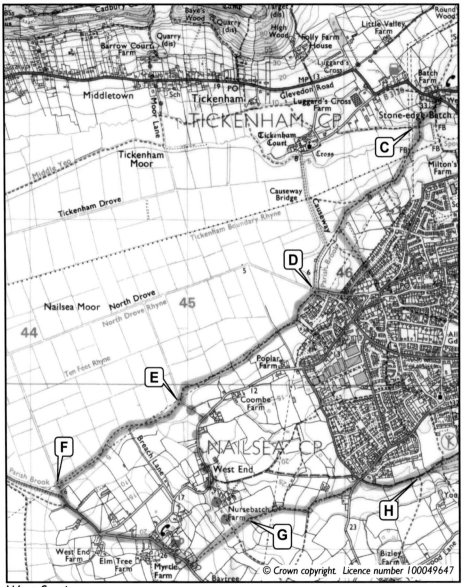

© Crown copyright. Licence number 100049647

West Section

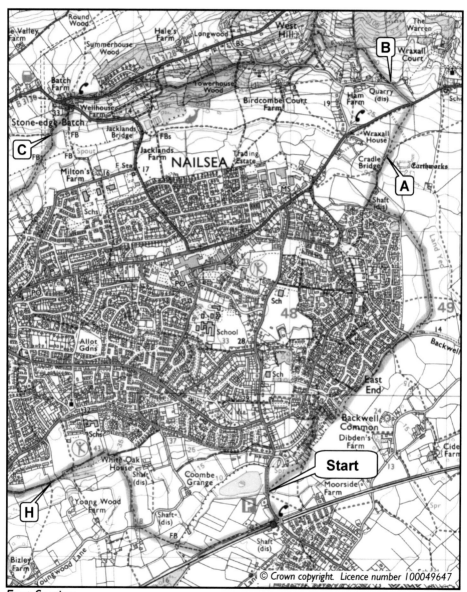

East Section

Backwell Lake to Backwell Bow

Leave the car park by the main entrance and go over the stile in the stone wall opposite. Go diagonally left across the field to the far corner, then over some stone steps and up to the road. Turn right and stay on the pavement. At the end of the grassy area on the left, cross the road and take the footpath between a wooden  fence on the right and a hedge on the left. At a brick wall turn right between two wooden fences. Cross Bucklands View and continue straight ahead. At a stone wall turn right, and continue with a wooden fence on the right. At a brick wall ignore the path to the left and continue straight on between two wooden fences.

On reaching an open grassy area, turn left. Ignore an open area on the left and continue straight on, past some large stones on the right, to a metal gate. Continue along the grassy area, keeping to the right of the brick house ahead. Near the end of the grassy area, bear right along a narrow track bordered on either side by tall bushes and onto the road (Backwell Bow).

Backwell Bow to Ham Lane

Cross the road, go through a kissing gate and follow the right-hand edge of the field. In about 100 m, just past a large oak tree, go through another gate on the right, and continue in the same direction with the hedge now on the left. Continue straight ahead, ignoring a path which crosses the route near a metal gate on the left. At the end of the field go through another gate and continue straight ahead with the hedge still on the left. In approximately 150 m go through a kissing gate on the left and go straight ahead towards the houses, keeping the hedge on the left. Where the hedge gives way to a ditch, do not cross the ditch but continue straight ahead, with the ditch on the left, to another hedge on the left. Shortly cross a wooden bridge on the left. Continue straight ahead for a short distance then bear right to path between two hedges. Where the path opens out into a wider grassy area, go up to the hedge which is straight ahead then turn right down a sunken track to a kissing gate.

Keep straight ahead with the hedge on the left, passing the ruins of Prideaux Coal Mine, one of the older mines in the area, on the right. Go through a metal gate and on to another metal gate on the far side of the field. Continue straight ahead to a wooden bridge with stiles at each end (Cradle Bridge).

Cradle Bridge is mentioned in the Churchwardens and Overseers Accounts Book of 1789-90, which ordered that the bridge, which carried an ancient burial road, should be repaired. Where the road led or where it came from, sadly, is not known. The original bridge was destroyed some years ago but would have consisted of wooden planks with sides that rose from the base forming a 'v' shape, so giving it its name.

Cross the track and go through a metal gate almost opposite to the right. Point **A**. Cross the field diagonally to the right, to the far corner by the road. Go through a kissing gate, cross the road with care, and go up the road opposite (Ham Lane).

(The path to the left before the kissing gate leads to Wraxall House and the Old Barn public house, for those in need of refreshment.)

Few buildings in the area have such a fascinating and turbulent history as Wraxall House. Although sections of the present house were built around 1600, Ewales de Wrockesbal (Wrockesbal is one of the many spelling of Wraxall) lived on this site as long ago as 1225.

Since then it has had many owners, among them James Edward Homer, a partner in the Nailsea Glassworks. During WW2, Admiral Hugh Tweedie, the head of Wraxall Home Guard, lived here and the house was designated an emergency hospital. It has since been used as a drug addiction clinic, the headquarters of a religious community, a residential home, a school for mentally handicapped children and a hotel.

Originally there was a mill within the grounds but a second one was built later and continued to grind corn until the turn of the last century. This was eventually demolished to make way for the widening of Wraxall Road. One of the outbuildings is now a popular public house, known as the Old Barn.

Ham Lane to Tower House Lane

As you go up the lane, there are good views to the left over Tickenham Church and beyond, and behind to Backwell Hill.

Where the lane bears round to the left go straight ahead over a stile to the right of a metal gate. Point **B**. Continue straight ahead, with the hedge on the right, to a metal gate. Go through the trees to the next field and continue on with the hedge and a stone wall on the right.

There are now good views to the left over Nailsea.

8

In the corner of the field climb a steep bank to a tarmac Lane (Stoney Steep). Turn left then almost immediately cross a stile on the right. Follow the waymarked path to another stile, passing a house a short distance away on the right. Take the path to the right through the trees to another stile. Keep straight ahead then bear left of a house and down a path with a hedge on the left and wall on the right. Continue between some bushes to a grassy area.

Turn left then almost immediately go through a gate on the left. Go down a path with a hedge on the left and low wall/bank on the right to a tarmac road. Go down this road, through a gate, and onto Tower House Lane. *Notice the carved, wooden bear on the right, on the corner.*

Tower House Lane to Stone Edge Batch

Turn right up Tower House Lane. Where the lane turns to the right continue straight ahead through a gate to Tower House Wood.

This wonderful ancient woodland was purchased by the Woodland Trust in 1992 with help from the Countryside Commission and Nailsea Town Council. The woodland is made up of oak, ash, field maple, beech, wych elm and birch trees, which are managed by a programme of long term coppicing to ensure a wide diversity of wildlife. Throughout the 16½ acres there is a mixture of undergrowth that includes hazel, hawthorn, blackthorn and holly.

In springtime the forest floor is a haze of colour with bluebells, ransoms (wild garlic) and wood anemones all vying for space. Other species often seen here include early purple orchids, lesser violets and primroses. Later in the year, many different types of fungi flourish on the dead and decaying wood.

Birdlife too abounds in the woods. Watch out for nuthatches, treecreepers, blue, great and long tailed tits, as well as the diminutive goldcrest, Britain's smallest bird. There is no shortage of larger birds either – wood peckers and jays are often seen flitting between trees, whilst buzzards and sparrow hawks hunt on the perimeter. This is also a good place to spot roe deer. Although reasonably abundant in the area, they are fairly shy, tending to do most of their grazing at dawn and dusk. A quiet approach and keen eyes may well produce a sighting of these beautiful creatures.

On entering the wood continue straight ahead, ignoring paths up to the right and down to the left. Eventually you will come to a wire fence on the right, which soon becomes a mixture of fence and hedge. Continue straight ahead with this boundary on the right. Where it turns to the right, follow the path round to the  right, keeping the boundary on the right until you pass between two large stones and onto a gravel lane.

Turn right and follow this lane up to the main road. Cross the road with care to the pavement opposite, and turn left towards the Tickenham Road.

Where the footpath is raised above the road, look for a green box, on the right, with the inscription "Bristol Water Works Company, Standpipe number 32; Only to be opened by those issued with a key". Boxes of this type date back to between 1910 and the late 1920s. The standpipes inside were generally for use of company or council staff needing a water supply when there were no hydrants available. They may even have been used at times to allow householders to collect water. They have not been used for many decades, but there are still a fair number buried under hedges, around North Somerset in particular.

On this section there are good views to the left over Nailsea and Backwell Hill, and straight ahead to Tickenham Church.

Before the junction cross the road with care to a grassy area, and continue down to the junction.

Stone Edge Batch to West End

Follow the pavement round to the left to a telephone box. Cross the road with great care and take the track almost immediately opposite and slightly to the left, down to a gate and a stile. Go down the field with the hedge/wall on the left. About half way down the field look for a stile in the fence on the opposite side of the field. Cross this stile, continue to another stile in the far corner of the field. and cross the river. Point **C**.

Go down the bank towards a gate by a small tree. Go through this gate then bear right towards the middle of the three nearest pylons, to a bridge over the rhyne. Continue straight ahead, to the right of the pylon, to the hedge, then turn right and follow the hedge, keeping the hedge on the left. Go through two gates and past some sheds on the left, then through a metal gate. Continue straight ahead with a stream on the left. Go over the next stile and on to a metal gate. Do not go through this gate, but turn left over a stile and a bridge. Continue straight ahead across the field to a stile to left of two red brick houses. Continue to the road and turn right.

At Hanham Way turn right and follow the old road. Cross the Causeway to a kissing gate to the left of the track (not the gate on the right-hand side of the track). Point **D**. Continue straight ahead with the rhyne on the left. Ignore an old stone stile with a circular hole, on the left, and continue straight ahead, keeping, the rhyne on the left.

After several fields, cross a stone stile and pass through small group of trees to where a track crosses the path, point **E**.

For a slightly shorter route (8¼ miles), which avoids the busy road through West End, follow the instructions at the end of this section.

For the main route, keep straight ahead across several fields for another kilometre (0.6 mile), ignoring another track to the left. Eventually you come to a track going to the left and the right, with no way ahead, with a stone arched bridge on the left and where the power cables cross the path. Point **F**. Take the track to the left, to the road.

Throughout the Middle Ages attempts were made to drain the moors and create additional agricultural land. The water, which drained off the surrounding limestone hills, always won, and Nailsea remained a narrow island for much of the year. During the nineteenth century the moors were successfully drained and the ground used for agriculture. Heavy prolonged rain, though, still floods the ground temporarily and gives at least a small glimpse of the past.

West End to Backwell Lake

Turn left and continue ahead past the Blue Flame, ignoring Nailsea Moor Lane and West End Lane to the left. Just past a large white house and a bungalow on the right, take the footpath on the left, between a fence and a stone wall. Go over a stile and down the left-hand side of the field to a stile and a small stream. Go to the right

around a small pond then diagonally left to a field gate on the skyline, point **C**. Cross a stone stile in the wall to the left of this gate. Keep to the left-hand edge of the field to a stile just past a barn on the left. Cross this stile and continue straight ahead along the farm track to the road. Turn left then take the track on the right opposite Engine Lane. Continue to the open scrubland on Morgan's Hill, point **H**.

Continue ahead along a well defined path to large gap in a hedge which crosses the path. Go through this gap then immediately bear right down to a gap in the hedge just left of an electricity pole. Descend through this gap to a track. Turn left then immediately right over a stile. Go down the right-hand side of the field, skirting around a small pond. Where the hedge bears away to the right continue straight ahead to a gate. At the road turn left then almost immediately right over a stile.

Bear diagonally left to a stile part way along the opposite field boundary. The path now goes through horse paddocks. The official path goes diagonally down the field, aiming to the left of an electric pole and a white house, to a concrete bridge and a gap in the hedge. However, it is advisable to follow the indicated route through the paddocks to avoid the horses. After crossing the bridge, continue straight ahead to a stile by a metal gate. At the lane turn left to the station. At the main road turn left back to Backwell Lake and the car park.

That Nailsea needed a railway link was never in any doubt. The mines could produce more coal than could be transported easily, leaving huge stockpiles. When the railway did finally come, in 1841, it was actually situated in the parish of Backwell, and being nearly two miles out of town had little impact. By the time tram links were built to some of the larger pits, the writing was on the wall for Nailsea coal, and the market had become flooded with cheaper coal from Bristol and Wales.

The line, which was originally broad gauge, was an extension of Brunel's Great Western Railway, and ran from Bristol to Exeter. The station has undergone many face-lifts since then, and is still heavily used for connections with Bristol and London Paddington.

Alternative route (8¼ miles)

From point **E** turn left over a concrete bridge and follow a track up to the road. Turn right along the road, taking care as it is very narrow. Ignore a path which goes up a concrete track to a farm on the left, near

a house called Windrush, and take the next path on the left, in about 50 m. Keep straight ahead across the field, past an electricity pole, and cross a stone stile in the wall on the far side. Bear left up the hill towards a pylon on the skyline, then bear left again towards a gate near a corner in the wall on the left, to rejoin the main round at point **G**.

LOOP WALK I

A history walk around Nailsea - 5 miles

This walk starts from Backwell Lake car park.

Nailsea has a fascinating history which can be explored with this easy walk. It includes the two earlier centres of Nailsea, as well as the 'new' town centre.

When the new town of Nailsea was built in the early 1970s, the excess runoff caused flooding further down the river Kenn. Backwell Lake was created in 1975 –76 as a balancing pond to reduce this problem.

Take the path on the left side of the lake and go clockwise round the lake. Cross over a concrete bridge, and a little further on go through a kissing gate hidden in the hedge on the left, near a noticeboard. Follow this path to a grassy area (Morgan's Hill). Go diagonally left uphill to the road (The Perrings). Continue along the left pavement to Youngwood Lane. Turn left, then almost immediately right along a path to the right of a house called Badgers Oak. Where the path forks, bear left to an open area and continue straight ahead along the top of the hill. Just after the path meets the hedge on the right and just before an oak tree, take the path to the right (the playing fields of the Grove are on the left). Follow this path, turning left at a metal gate, then almost immediately right keeping the school on the right, to the road (St. Mary's Grove). Cross with care and take the path opposite. At the end of this turn left, then right into the churchyard.

This was the first centre of Nailsea. Little has actually survived of the medieval village, described by Margaret Thomas as probably a cluster of hovels and cottages around Holy

15

Trinity church. The church dates from the 13th century, but was a chapelry of the parish of Wraxall until 1811. The corner pinnacles were added to the tower in 1904. Note the porch, which is tiled with Pennant Sandstone.

Bear diagonally left and leave the churchyard through a gate to a small road.

Opposite is the Tithe Barn, which dates from about the same time, although it has been altered over the years, having been used not only to store the tithes (the tenth paid to the church) but much later as a school.

Turn right and follow the road, then bear left in front of a row of cottages, and continue round to the right and to a road (Queens Road). Cross with care and continue straight ahead into a lane. Turn left at the end then right at a T junction, keeping a row of willow trees on your left (Union Street).

On the right is Tall Cottage, a three storey converted engine house. This area, Kingshill, was the second centre of Nailsea, which became important when coal was worked here from the 15th century.

At a T junction on a bend, turn left into North Street. Carry straight on, noting Old Fire Station Court on the right. Continue past the end of Queens Road and Hanham Way, and take the second turn on the right into North Lane. On the left is another three storey converted engine house. Just past this house, turn left into a small lane between two stone walls. Go through a white metal gate to No. 8. Where the tarmac drive ends, keep straight ahead through a small orchard, with a tall hedge on the left. At the end turn left, then bear right over a bridge and a lovely stone stile. Turn right.

Look across the fields to the higher land beyond, which is Cadbury Camp, an Iron Age hill fort, the oldest known settlement in the area, dating from about 4000 years ago.

Follow the river to the road. Cross with care to the narrow lane opposite between two hedges (Watery Lane). At Hanham Way and Causeway View, keep straight ahead ignoring these two roads.

This area is Kingshill the early centre of coal mining. As miners moved to this area, it gradually replaced the area around the church as the focus of the village . Near the site of the former green and duckpond in the centre of Kingshill is the oldest pub in Nailsea, now called the Moorend Spout, said to date from 1735

At the T junction opposite the Corner Stores, cross Silver Street with care.. It was named because for much of the year water flowed along it, making it look silver. Turn left and just after number 18, take the footpath on the right between two stone walls.

It was in this area that coal was first worked in Nailsea, because it outcrops very close to the surface. Look carefully in the gardens on the right for evidence of coal. Opposite the end of the path was one of the first Wesleyan Methodist chapels in the area, dating from 1792 (now Nailsea Social Club).

At the end turn left and follow the road round to the right past the car park of the social club. Just after Chapel Barton, take a drive to the right by no. 18. Just before the drive ends, take a path to the left and follow this to a road. Cross with care and take the path straight ahead. At the next road, turn left, and cross with care. In a short distance take a path on the right just past a cottage with a small, round window. At the end of this path, bear right and follow into Ashton Crecent. At the T junction turn left (Hazelbury Road) and continue ahead. Follow this road, ignoring all side roads. At the T junction cross the main road with care and keep right towards the car park. Follow the path left then right round the edge of the car park to the town centre and Library

In 1958, it was proposed that Nailsea should be developed as a new town, to concentrate new building in the northern part of Somerset. After much opposition, this was finally passed in 1970, and this new town centre was built adjacent to the old village green and High Street where there were shops, pubs etc. which had supplied the needs of the glassworkers.

Go straight ahead through Somerset Square, bearing right at the far side. At the High Street, turn left. At a T-junction keep straight ahead, passing the Royal Oak on the right. At the next junction, cross the road at the lights and go down the slope or steps to Tesco. Turn right passing the entrance* and continue on the pavement towards the garage. Cross the pedestrian crossing into the park and turn left to the entrance to the play area.

There is an interesting display with more details about glassmaking in Nailsea near the car park – turn left beyond the entrance and it is on the wall of the building in the car park.

This area is the old glassworks site. In 1788, John Lucas, who had previously been associated with glassmaking in Bristol, set up a new glassworks on Nailsea Heath. There were two glass cones making green glass for window glass, bottles and other household items. Outside normal working hours the glassblowers used the green

glass with white glass bought from another works (each only made one colour) to make decorative items such as pipes and paperweights - there is an excellent collection on display at Clevedon Court. The works extended from the long low building on the other side of the road on the left (a later addition, the rolling mill) across the site of Tesco and the car park to the three storey building on the right, now the Masonic Hall but formerly the manager's house. At the back of the car park on the right is a row of glassworkers' cottages, built to a high standard for the well paid workers.

Coal is needed to make glass, and this was mined in Nailsea. At the back of the play area on the right is a well preserved coal mine. A horse walked round the circular whim to raise coal from the shaft.

Just past the play area bear left into the corner and through the gate with stone pillars. Cross the road with care.

The overgrown area ahead is a more typical remains of coal mining in Nailsea. Coal was dug from shallow seams, and the spoil heaps like this one left as evidence of the mining.

Continue straight ahead across the grassy area with a hedge on the right and past the spoil heap on the left. On reaching a road continue straight ahead for a short distance to a tarmac path. Turn right between two wooden fences. Continue to the school and playing fields and keep straight ahead on the tarmac path with the fields on the right. On reaching a road turn right and follow it round to the left. At the end of the hedge on the right by a low brick wall, bear diagonally right across the fields to a gap in the hedge just to the left of a large oak tree. Bear diagonally right to a path just to the right of the last house. Carry straight on into the wood to where the path forks. Bear left, then straight over a path which crosses. Follow the path as it bears right into the quarry

Here Pennant Sandstone, found in this area with Coal Measures, was quarried. It was used to build many of the older houses in Nailsea and was particularly suitable for roofing because it could be easily made into flat slates, as used on the porch of Holy Trinity Church.

At the quarry face, turn left, then left again to follow a sunken track out of the quarry. At the top turn right to a field.

On the right in the grassy area in front of the school is part of the raised bank on which the tramway which carried stone from the quarry was built.

Cross the field to a gap in the trees, then go straight on with the croquet clubhouse on the right. At the end of the croquet lawn, turn right and follow the path to Station Road. Turn left and follow the pavement down to Backwell Lake.

LOOP WALK 2

Truckle Wood and Watercress Farm - 5½ miles

Starting from Backwell Lake, this walk skirts around the East of Nailsea before climbing the hill behind Wraxall, to give good views over Nailsea and Backwell Hill. It then descends through Truckle Wood, where there are bluebells in the spring, passes the beautifully restored Watercress Farm, and returns across fields to the start.

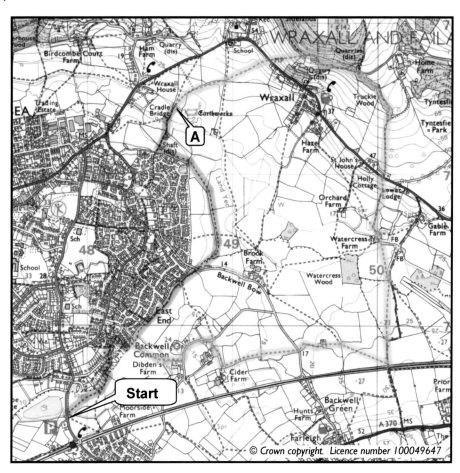

© Crown copyright. Licence number 100049647

From Backwell lake follow the main Round to point **A**. After crossing the track do not go diagonally to the right, as on the main Round, but bear further diagonally to the right, to where the hedge bends away to the right. On reaching the hedge, shortly go through a gate on the right

and continue in the same direction with the hedge now on the left. Cross a stile in the corner of the field then immediately left over another stile. Go diagonally up the field to a stile in the wall just to the left of the old school house. Cross the road with care to some steps up to a kissing gate. Go diagonally right up the hill. Cross a stile

part way up the hill and continue on up to a stile in the far right-hand corner of the field.

As you go up the hill look back occasionally at the view over Nailsea and beyond.

Go over the stile then left up through the trees to a path. Turn right along this path, with a stone wall on the right, and go behind the white house. On reaching a tarmac drive turn left. Continue along this drive, ignoring a drive which goes down to the right. Just past the mast on the left, follow a path on the right which goes down through the woods. Cross a track which goes down to the field on the right and continue straight ahead through the wood. On emerging from the wood, turn right down a broad track to the road.

Cross the road with care to a stile opposite, then follow the fence downhill, to a stile and onto a tarmac drive. Turn right towards Watercress Farm. Where the path divides, take the left fork which goes in front of the farm house. Go past large double gates leading into the farm house, and continue by the wall as it turns to the right. Go through a gap in the wall and continue between the restored barn on the left and the farm house on the right, keeping a stone wall on the left. Keep straight ahead through a gate and cross a bridge over the river to a stile. Bear left to the far left-hand corner of the field. Cross a stile then go diagonally right to the far right-hand corner of the field, then over a stile into a lane. Turn right and follow the lane to the cycleway.

The railway bridge ahead is a good place to watch the steam trains that occasionally run on this line.

Do not go over the railway bridge but turn right along the cycleway, then immediately through a kissing gate on the right. Go diagonally across the field to the opposite corner. Go over a stile then bear left to a corner, which is to the left of a barn. Cross a bridge then turn right, keeping the field boundary on the right and a small copse on the left, to a gate on the right. Go through this gate then bear left to a stile and onto the road.

Turn left then almost immediately right over a stile in a wide hedge. Go straight ahead keeping the hedge on the left at first. Where the hedge bears away to the left, continue straight ahead, aiming for a pair of electric poles a couple of fields ahead, and pass to the right of a large oak tree to reach a stile in the hedge ahead.

Note: at the time of writing you are welcome to walk in this plantation, by kind permission of the owner.

Cross this stile and continue straight ahead with the hedge on the left. Cross another stile and continue to double gates leading onto a tarmac track. Turn right along this track to a lane, then right again for a short distance to reach the road. Turn left and follow the road for about 500 m. Just before a long, low barn, cross a stile on the right and follow the left-hand edge of the field. Go through a gate then round the right-hand edge of the field towards the houses in Nailsea. On reaching the corner turn left and in about 50 m right over a bridge to rejoin the Round. Turn left and retrace your steps back to the start.

LOOP WALK 3

Tower House Wood and Moor End Spout - 5 miles

From the lay-by at the bottom of Tower House Lane, this walk climbs the hill to give good views over Nailsea and beyond. It then passes through the secluded Tower House Wood, before descending to the Land Yeo River. After passing Tickenham Church it returns to the start via Moor End Spout. In the spring there are bluebells in Tower House Wood and daffodils in the MacMillan Cancer Support Field of Hope.

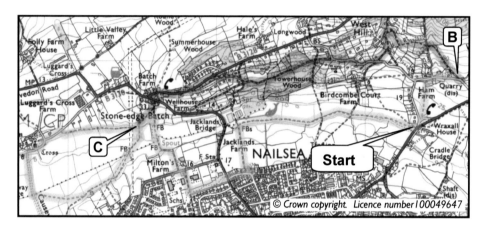

© Crown copyright. Licence number 100049647

This walk starts from the lay-by at the bottom of Tower House lane. It may also be started from Clevedon Road by starting at the appropriate point in the directions below. During the winter or after heavy rain, parts of the walk may be wet and muddy.

Go through a metal gate where the lay-by meets Tower House lane and continue straight ahead across the field to a wooden fence on the far side, to the left of a white house. Cross a stile, by a willow tree, into a garden and bear right up a short slope to a tarmac lane outside Ham Farm. Turn right along this narrow lane, ignoring Stoney Steep on the left. Just before the lane turns sharp right, with a concrete track going up on the left, cross a stile on the left, to the right of a metal gate, to join the main round at point **B**.

25

Follow the Main Round to point **C**.

After crossing the river, do not go down the bank, but turn right along the bank for 500 m, to a road. Turn left, then left again at a T-junction in front of the church, and follow the road towards Nailsea, shortly leaving the church behind. *The road is very narrow and can be busy at times, so take great care.* Immediately after a bridge with white parapets, cross a stile on the left and go diagonally across the field to the far corner.

This section may be very wet underfoot after heavy rain.

In the next field go to the left of the farm buildings, to a kissing gate in the right-hand corner. Continue straight ahead with the rhyne on the right and go through a kissing gate just past the first set of overhead cables, and continue straight on. Where the rhyne bears away to the right, keep straight ahead to a bridge over the river, just to the right of the left-hand pylon, then bear right to a gate to the right of a solitary tree. Go straight ahead up the bank of the river and cross a stile which was crossed earlier. Bear right to a stile in a wire fence, then bear right again down to a bridge over the river. Descend the river bank to a stile on the right and go through the bushes to a bridge at Moor End Spout. Continue straight ahead with the rhyne on the left to a stile on the left, then follow the lane to the road (Pound Lane). Turn left and in a short distance take a path on the right which runs between two schools. On reaching an open area, take the tarmac path on the left to Clevedon Road, near the ambulance station.

In the spring there is a wonderful display of daffodils here, in the Field of Hope.

Cross the road and continue along Greenfield Crescent.

26

Take the path on the left, opposite Valley Way Road. On reaching a field, turn left to a stile in the corner, then right down the right-hand edge of the field to bridge in the corner. Turn right and follow the path and a track along the river back to the start.

LOOP WALK 4

Cadbury Camp - 6 miles

Starting from Clevedon Road car park, this walk goes to Moor End Spout and on past Tickenham Church, before climbing to the iron age hill fort of Cadbury Camp. Here there are fabulous views across the Bristol Channel to Wales, Steepholm, Crook Peak and Backwell Hill. It returns past the large impressive houses of Cadbury Camp lane and the lakes at Jacklands Bridge. Look out for the waterwheel at Tickenham Weir Mill.

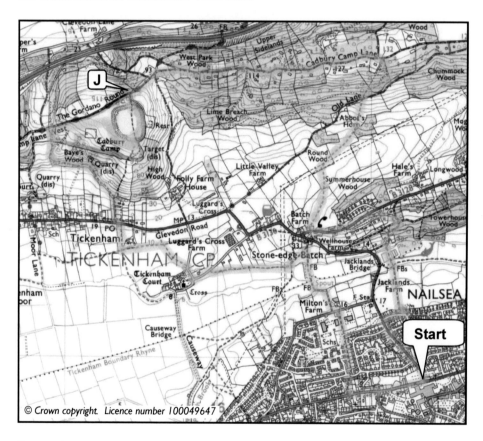

© Crown copyright. Licence number 100049647

From Clevedon Road car park turn right along Stockway North and on into Silver Street. Just past a row of cream coloured houses set back from the road, take a footpath on the right. Cross over Westway and continue straight ahead eventually going over a grassy area and between two schools to a road (Pound Lane). Turn left and in a short distance take a track on the right signed Moor End Spout and Tickenham. Follow this track as it bends round to the left to a stile adjacent to a metal gate. Turn right and follow the field boundary down to a bridge at Moor End Spout. Continue straight ahead to a stile. Climb the river bank, cross a bridge and continue up hill with a hedge on the right. About half way up the field look for a stile in the fence on the opposite side of the field. Cross this stile, go down to another stile in the far corner of the field and re-cross the river.

Turn right along the river bank towards Tickenham church for about 500 m, to a road. Turn left to a T-junction in front of the church. Turn right and follow the road with care for about 100 m to a stile on the left, where the road bends sharply to the right. Go straight ahead through the trees to another stile. Bear diagonally right across the field to a bridge in the middle of the opposite boundary. Do not cross this bridge, but turn left along the river bank.

Just before Tickenham Weir Mill look, for the water wheel underneath the house.

In the corner of the field, just before the gate into the next field, turn right over a stile hidden under the trees and set back over a bridge. Continue straight ahead to a stile then up an enclosed path to the road. Cross the road and turn left, then almost immediately, just past number 219, take a path on the right between wooden fences. On reaching a stile turn left, with a garden fence on the left. Continue on this path as it goes through scrubland and into a wood.

Along this section there are good views to the left across Tickenham and on to Worlebury Hill, Crook Peak and Backwell Hill.

Follow the path along the edge of the wood, eventually turning right uphill. Where the path forks, keep left and on up to a stile straight ahead. Cross this stile into National Trust land and continue straight ahead, with the field boundary on the left, to a stile in the corner. At this point one can either go immediately along Cadbury Camp Lane, or visit the iron-age hill fort of Cadbury Camp. To go immediately along Cadbury Camp Lane, cross the stile and turn right. Follow the lane and pick-up the directions from point **J** below.

To visit the iron-age hill fort, do not cross the stile, but turn right along the centre of the field towards the horizon.

As you go up the hill there are good views behind to Crook Peak, Worlebury Hill, Flat Holm and Steep Holm.

On reaching the fort, turn right along the outer embankment to where there is a bench slightly downhill to the right before the bushes. Look for a path on the left which goes down into the ditch and up the embankment. Follow the inner bank to the right, to the corner of the field  diametrically opposite, where a farm track goes through a large gap through both embankments. Turn right down a path to a stile and onto Cadbury Camp Lane, point **J**. Turn right down a stony track which eventually becomes a tarmac lane.

Continue along this lane, past large houses on the left and right, for about 1200 m. Just past a long stone wall and a house called South Fall, on the right, go over a wooden step stile with a metal hoop handrail, on the right.

Follow the path between a wooden fence on the right and a wire fence on the left. Where the fences separate, follow the fence on the right, which becomes a wire fence, as it bears round to the right. Eventually the path turns away from the fence to follow a slightly sunken route, with an old post and wire fence on the left. On reaching a stile bear slightly  right down the field towards the right-hand end of a belt of trees straight ahead. On nearing the trees, bear right again in the direction of the left-hand one of two pylons to a stile. (Not the two pylons immediately on the left.) Bear left to a stile near a metal gate part way along the left-hand hedge. Go straight ahead to a metal gate, then continue in the same direction, up a slope towards a red tiled roof. Follow a short track to a stile and a road, Tickenham Hill.

Turn left and take the second turning on the right, Stonehenge Lane. Follow this stony lane down, ignoring a tarmac path up to the left. Where the lane turns sharp right by some large stones, take the path straight ahead down through the trees to a high step into an open area. *(This section is steep, and can be slippery in wet weather and in the autumn, due to leaves.)* Continue straight ahead through a grassy area and go between the ponds. Cross two bridges into field. Continue up the left-hand edge of the field to a stile on the left in the corner. Turn right by a tall metal fence to a road, Greenfield Crescent. Turn right to Clevedon Road then left back to the car park

LOOP WALK 5

Backwell and Nailsea Ponds - 4½ miles

From Backwell Lake this walk crosses fields, where there are views towards Brockley, to Backwell West Town It then skirts round Grove Farm before passing Nailsea Ponds, where it crosses the railway line. From Youngwood Lane, where there are views of Chelvey Church and Nailsea Court, it climbs gently to Morgan's Hill, for views over Backwell and Chelvey. Look out for water lilies, dragon flies and tadpoles at Nailsea Ponds.

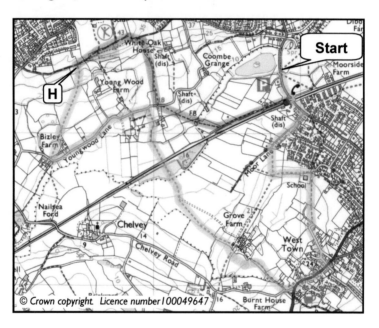

© Crown copyright. Licence number100049647

Turn right out of the car park and go along the main road towards Backwell. Just past the railway bridge turn right into Moor Lane. Where the road forks at Long Thorn, take the right-hand fork, Moor Lane. On reaching a sharp right-hand bend, go straight ahead through a kissing gate and continue straight up the field to the far hedge. On reaching the hedge, stay in this field and turn left to a kissing gate in the corner. Follow the tarmac path straight ahead, bearing right where it meets another path, and eventually going between the school on the right and houses on the left. At the road turn right up towards the school. Go through a gate to the left of the school gate and along a short path with a hedge on the right and a wire fence on the left. At the end go through a gate and continue in the same direction along a short track with a hedge on the right and tall, wooden fence on the left. At the end of the track, bear slightly left to a kissing gate just left of a metal gate. Bear left across the next field to a gate which leads onto a narrow lane. Go straight ahead and follow the lane as it turns left. Shortly take the right fork to the main road (A370). Turn right along the pavement for about 250 m, then right into Chelvey Road.

Note the Victorian drinking trough on the corner.

After about 50 m take a narrow lane on the right. Just before the lane turns right in front of the farm, go through a kissing gate on the left and in about 30 m through another kissing gate on the right.

Go round the edge of the farm yard on the right to a kissing gate in the far hedge. Continue round the farm yard to another kissing gate at the back of the farm. Turn left down the hill to a kissing gate in the far hedge, leaving the farm behind. Continue straight ahead to a gate and wooden bridge in the far left-hand corner. Bear right towards some trees between two electricity poles. Go through a metal gate and continue straight ahead to a bridge over a small stream, and on through Nailsea Ponds to the railway line.

The ponds were originally excavated to provide material for the railway embankment.

Climb the steps up the embankment and cross the railway with great care. Do not attempt to cross if a train is in sight, however far away it may be, but retreat down the embankment until it has passed. Continue ahead with the rhyne on the left and cross a stile on the left near the far corner. Turn right to another stile immediately in the corner. Go along the right-hand field boundary to a stile in the corner. Bear slightly left to a stile adjacent to a metal gate in the far hedge.

Turn left along Youngwood lane. Ignore a footpath on the right opposite Deerhurst Farm.

Along this section there are good views of Nailsea Court and later Chelvey Church.

After about 600 m, immediately after the lane turns sharp right opposite Cherry Orchard Farm, take the footpath on the right up some stone steps in the wall. Go diagonally left across the field to the far corner, just left of some stone buildings. Continue in the same direction to a stile adjacent to a metal gate, then diagonally across the next field to another stile adjacent to a metal gate. Bear left up the slope to a stile in the middle of the far hedge, to join the main Round at point **H**. Follow the main Round back to the start.

LOOP WALK 6

Parish Brook and North Drove - 3¼ miles

This walk crosses Nailsea Moor, firstly by following The Parish Brook, then returning to the start along North Drove, which was designated as a bridleway in 2009. There is an abundance of wildlife; you may see swans, herons and buzzards, and, if you are lucky, deer. In the spring and summer wild flowers abound.

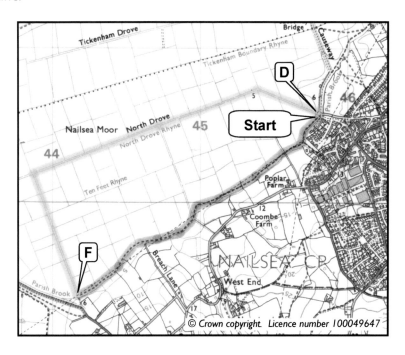

The walk starts at the junction of Hanham way and the Causeway, point **D**. Follow the main Round from point **D** to point **F**. At point **F** do not take the track to the left as for the main Round, but take the track to the right. After 900 m, at a T-junction, turn right and follow the track back to the start, ignoring a track to the right just before a metal barn.

NAILSEA & DISTRICT FOOTPATH GROUP

Formed in 1975, the principal aim of the Group was, and still is, to encourage people to walk the definitive Rights of Way in Nailsea and adjacent parishes, and to enjoy the countryside. In so doing the Group has contributed to the preservation, protection and maintenance of precious, often ancient, footpaths, so frequently under threat.

Our programme of walks offers a range of whole day, half day, weekend and weekday walks of varying distances and degrees of difficulty. The walks range from 2 mile easy strolls to 15 mile more strenuous walks. Many walks are local but we add interest and variety to the programme by including areas such as the Mendips, the Cotswolds, the Quantocks, the Welsh hills and even Devon. To explore further afield we include weekends in the UK and longer trips abroad. The programme is published regularly, and posters in local libraries and notice boards also advertise the walks.

The Group has around 150 members, of varying abilities. New members, of all ages, are always welcome. We are happy for potential members to walk with the Group on two occasions before deciding whether to join. We recommend that all walkers are equipped with waterproof walking footwear, appropriate clothing for seasonal weather and their own first-aid kits. Our leaders can and will advise where necessary.

The membership fee is currently £4 per year. The Group has third party public liability insurance. Members need to insure privately for accidental injury.

We look forward to you joining us for many rewarding, healthy experiences.